EXCUSE ME AS I KISS THE SKY

POEMS BY

Rudy Francisco

Button Publishing Inc.

Minneapolis

2023

EXCUSE ME AS I KISS THE SKY
POETRY
AUTHOR: Rudy Francisco
EDITOR: Sam Van Cook
COVER DESIGN: Patricia(PK) Kobusingye

◇

◇

Published by Button Poetry
Minneapolis, MN 55418 | http://www.buttonpoetry.com

◇

Manufactured in the United States of America
PRINT ISBN: 978-1-63834-077-5
EBOOK ISBN: 978-1-63834-078-2
AUDIOBOOK ISBN: 978-1-63834-079-9

First printing

EXCUSE ME AS I KISS THE SKY

TABLE OF CONTENTS

V. Question-and-Answer

VI. Free Verse

VII. Page to Stage

VIII. Love Poems

EXCUSE ME AS I
KISS THE SKY

THIS SONG MAKES ME CRY. WANNA HEAR IT?

It begins like it doesn't want to interrupt
your day but needs a few minutes of your time.
Acappella, so the music notes hold their breath until they pass out,
silence breaking their fall. Her voice, a stampede of sunflowers
trampling my anxiety. I breathe, I close both eyes, loneliness
dissipates, and I let the song drive me home. Maybe all the things
we've been through exist somewhere inside a melody.

I.

ODE

"Glory to the undertow and the way new love will dance in it, the churn that brings everything to the surface. Shout for the resilience of everything we had to go through to bring us here. Make a joyful noise that we are here. We didn't capsize when we thought we would. Didn't drown when we thought we would."

— JUNIOUS "JAY" WARD, "AN ODE TO WHAT THE DIVORCE DIDN'T TAKE"

ODE

A traditional and ancient poetic form, the ode strives to bridge the gap from the ordinary to the transcendent. In its best execution, the ode brings into focus and celebrates everyday details and experiences.

Generally, the ode is centered on a specific object or experience, or else a universal class of objects or experiences: the summer day, the green of a lover's eyes, a sleeping baby.

Historically, odes tended to be governed by strict forms, and while these traditional formal odes are still written, free verse odes are more common today.

I love performing. Sometimes, I'll do a question-and-answer session with the audience. I believe that being able to dialogue with the attendees allows the engagement to surpass entertainment and transition into a more shared, transformative experience for everyone involved, including myself. Some of my favorite events are the ones where I've been able to have discussions about poetry, writing, performance, and the impact it all has on the world.

So, one time, I'm doing a Q&A session at a university. Most of the questions were the typical inquiries—"How did you get started?", "What's your favorite poem?", "What's your process?", etc.—I get these questions often, so I could respond with ease.

After fielding the questions, I'm signing books, talking to students, taking pictures, and as I'm about to leave, a young man approaches like he was apprehensive about claiming more of my time. We were wearing similar outfits—a knit sweater, button-up shirt, and Jordans. His hands and voice were slightly shaking. He asked if I could answer one more question before I left. I complimented his cardigan, responding, "Of course."

He said, "I don't think I have enough sadness to be a good poet. Should I just give up on writing?"

I was surprised by the question and asked for clarification.

He said, "I'm happy. I haven't always been, but I am now. I'm in a really good place, but who wants to hear a poem about that?"

I told him, "There is space in this craft for every emotion and feeling. Don't be pressured into writing about sadness that you don't have. Artists who transcend are not those who fit inside a mold; they're ones who challenge craft and push boundaries.

We don't see a lot of poems about happiness because when we are happy, we're just out being happy; we're usually not thinking about writing poems. Sadness often convinces us to isolate, forcing us to be alone with our thoughts. Writing happens in these moments because we're having a lot of feelings, and we aren't occupied. Poems about sadness are important. They are cathartic and help us process heavy emotions. Poems about happiness are equally important."

I appreciate odes because they provide the opportunity to highlight anything. I choose something or someone that makes me joyful, and I brainstorm why it's important to me, focusing on how it makes me feel and why I need it to exist. I like to interact with the subtleties of a subject. Sometimes, the poem functions as a dialogue between myself and the subject, and other times, I take a more narrative approach to tell a story about the subject. Odes can be a creative way to discuss important things around us.

ODE TO MY MOTHER'S PLANTAINS

In my version of heaven, my mother's plantains fall from the sky every Wednesday afternoon. A sweet rain with burnt edges. All the drops have been cut longways and fried for five minutes. In the afterlife, this is the only event on my calendar. I step onto the balcony at 11:59 a.m., palms up, waiting for the showers. I asked God to put taste buds on the insides of my hands so I can enjoy each one twice.

ODE TO THE FRESH HAIRCUT

There's something remarkable about you. Maybe it's the clean edges or the flawless line up. Perhaps the taper or the way the fade sunset-blends from a Number 3 until skin. You turn all surfaces into mirrors, and we search for ourselves on everything shiny enough to hold a reflection. You're a reminder that our aunties weren't lying when they kissed us on the face and said we were handsome. You hostage all my camera-shy, make me want to be seen from every angle. Bless the harmony of freshly oiled clippers. Bless the straight razor's accuracy. Bless the rubbing alcohol and whatever they spray on our heads before we leave the chair. My barber once told me that, as a kid, he wanted to be an architect or a magician. "Congratulations," I replied. "Somehow, you found a way to become both."

ODE TO THE CARDIGAN

You are the best thing about September. The time of year when summer packs the rest of its belongings, fall subleases the breeze, and cold becomes a house guest with bad manners—shows up without warning, stays too long, and doesn't understand social cues very well. Autumn is slowly gentrifying all the trees, and this is your moment, old friend. Patron saint of buttons and cotton. You, archangel of the versatile garment. Of sneakers and jeans, dress shoes and slacks. Ready for any occasion. When Bruce Lee said, *Be like water*, you took that personally.

ODE TO OLD SPICE COLOGNE

I was only ten years old, but I must have smelled like I worked all day, like a whole shift with no breaks. I must have smelled like this job doesn't pay me enough, like my coworkers get on my nerves and the boss has less experience than I do. I probably smelled like my kids don't appreciate the sacrifices I make, like they don't keep their rooms clean, like they want McDonald's but don't have McDonald's money. I think I smelled like I would stand next to your car and help you back out of a parking spot, like I read the paper and call new music *noise*. I'm pretty sure I smelled like I grill better than you, like the meat on my BBQ ribs always falls off the bone when you lift them, like I make my own sauces, like I watch people try them and say, "That's good, ain't it?" I probably smelled like I pay taxes, change my own oil, and answer all questions with a story. I know I smelled like a dad or an uncle or just a man that didn't leave.

ODE TO SUMMER

Today, the sun decided to act all the way up. Showed out like it knew we were watching. Today, the weather refuses to lie; it's been 100° all week, and my sweat glands are having a little trouble dealing with the truth. But what I know is that, of all the things that want to kill me, the temperature is the least likely to succeed. So, I wipe my forehead, press a cold beverage to my lips, and I watch the sky slip into something more comfortable, something that will make the clouds wish they didn't have to leave so soon.

II.

OBIT

"Sometimes all I have
are words and to write them means
they are no longer
prayers but are now animals.
Other people can hunt them."

— VICTORIA CHANG, "TANKAS"

OBIT

A poem in the form of an obituary. While obituary poetry is not new, the modern "Obit" style was popularized by Victoria Chang and usually takes an unconventional approach to obituary writing. The obit poem is an ode to something surprising or out of the ordinary (confidence, doubt, appetite, a house, a laptop, a phone) that has died, no longer exists, or has been damaged. These poems often explore and transform the boundaries of personhood, grief, and attachment.

The modern obit reflects the structure of the newspaper obituary but subverts the obituary's linear narrative in favor of an expressive and interpretive approach to processing and documenting loss.

While talking to a fellow poet and friend, Aman Batra, I asked what she had been reading and if she had any recommendations for me. Aman excitedly mentioned that she had just finished *Obit* by Victoria Chang and said, "You will love it."

After reading *Obit*, I knew I had to try this form. I started by choosing something in my life that no longer existed. I picked an approximate date that it *died* to introduce the poem. I used the rest of the poem to discuss how I felt about the subject, memories I had, and how it had shaped my experience.

Growing up, I went to a lot of funerals. A few aunts and uncles, couple cousins and friends, and my grandmother. When you experience so much loss at such a young age, you realize how finite our time on Earth really is. I learned how to celebrate people while they are here, and to continue celebrating them when they are not. I learned that when people are no longer alive, they can still be present and that memories keep them with you.

The obit challenges us to understand everything around as living, breathing things with a beginning and an end. The obit is a brilliant way to commemorate the end.

died suddenly on April 3rd, 2016, at the age of thirty-three. My daughter came into this world the same way an orchid springs from the earth. The word *perfect* was born from the belly of Latin, a language of beginnings; *perficere*, which means complete. When her eyes bloomed, I realized that I've been an obtuse angle my entire life, and things were finally coming full circle. When I held her for the first time, my bones unlatched, I stashed my fangs, and then blunted my jagged edges until smooth. I looked at her and said, *all this tenderness is for you. I am yours.* My entire chest is a morning, a sunrise, a new day.

died on September 4th, 2020, at the age of twenty-three. An eviction notice is a lot heavier than it looks. Seems like it's just paper and ink, but it's all dead weight. Once, I carried my drunk friend up three flights of stairs, and I was sore for five days. That was so much easier than putting my father's war medals into a brown box and taping it closed. I treated my teenage home like a swordfish, waited for it to stop breathing and then scraped the insides clean. I packed a decade into the storage unit, threw away the rest, and watched a dump truck take all the memories we couldn't find space for. This is a special kind of betrayal, an unforgivable treason. I don't know who I should apologize to first.

OUR RELATIONSHIP

died quietly on February 10th, 2012. I realized that we hadn't had an actual conversation in months. You don't call me on your way home anymore, and I don't know anything new about your crazy coworkers. I tell a joke and you wouldn't even laugh. Often, I caught you staring off into space. I didn't interrupt because you seemed so peaceful away from the monotony of us. When something becomes routine, you can carve out all the emotion and just do it without thinking. Dialogue transformed into one-word answers, date night felt unnecessary, and we were just two satellites suffering in the same orbit. We didn't even know how unhappy we were because feeling anything was a waste of battery. Lonely in a relationship is the worst brand of grief, like planning a funeral for someone who still gets out of bed every morning.

MY PATIENCE

died violently on May 25th, 2020. The video of George Floyd's murder went viral. Once again, America found the ghost of Martin Luther King, Jr., dragged it out of the basement, and told us not to retaliate with violence. They say, *we are in the ocean looking for the water.* They say, *you don't see all this justice? All this equality? All this freedom?* The flag still mispronounces your name, but it is getting closer. The bald eagle apologized for sticking its claws into your flesh; the bird thought you were already dead, it was an honest mistake, and nobody's perfect. They say, *these incidents have nothing to do with color; it's not always about race; your ancestors would trade spots with you in a heartbeat, and we would allow them to talk just long enough to call it a blessing.* This country likes to wipe its mouth with our sorrow and then remind us of all the *progress* we've made. Meanwhile, white privilege is somewhere pointing at a picture of Colin Kaepernick and laughing.

MY HOOP DREAMS

died unexpectedly on April 8th, 2010, at the age of twenty-four. Survived by a pair of gray Kobe 9's and a Wilson Evolution basketball. Sports kept many neighborhood kids out of trouble; my brother decided to pass that savior down to me. I was taught the subtle art of shooting a jump shot when I was six years old. Bend the knees, tuck the elbow, follow through, and snap the wrist. Let it hang in the air if you're feeling fancy, yell *Jordan* on the fadeaway, smile when the ball goes in and hits nothing but the lowest part of the net. A ritual I still perform at least twice a week. In my spring, I made fun of the older men who just played for the cardio and moved like cold maple syrup. Now, I'm almost winter, and the waffles are ready. Today, I told my body to run faster. My legs acted like they didn't hear me.

III.

GOLDEN SHOVEL

"We stood in the road, and my father talked about jazz,
how sometimes a tune is born of outrage."

— TERRANCE HAYES, "THE GOLDEN SHOVEL"

GOLDEN SHOVEL

A contemporary and celebrated form, the golden shovel was invented and popularized in the book *Lighthead*, by Terrance Hayes, which won the National Book Award for Poetry. The form was initially used to celebrate and explore the writing of Gwendolyn Brooks while also creating poems that are in conversation with her work.

The golden shovel is constructed by selecting a specific quote or line and then writing a poem in which the final word of each line is the next word in the given quote.

The golden shovel is one of the first forms I explored. The first one I'd read was by Imani Cezanne, a poet who is pretty much my sister. During the pandemic, she began to explore form and wanted to show me what she came up with. The poem was incredible, and I loved the idea immediately. I was fascinated by the constraint of the form. It forces you to find creativity while keeping within the confines of the quote that you choose as the building block.

I attempted to write one, and I realized that it was much harder than it looked. I tried writing a poem and going back to incorporate the quote, but that didn't work. Next, I wrote the quote vertically and tried to write the poem line by line. That also did not work. After trial and error, I found a middle ground: I first picked a quote, decided on a general direction for the poem, and then pieced it all together. This form challenged me in ways that I have never experienced before, and it provided a gateway for me to explore more ways to approach the craft while also piquing my interest in poetic forms.

"EVERYBODY DIES, BUT NOT EVERYBODY LIVES" — DRAKE

I'm usually the person sitting alone. The one that **everybody**
asks if they're having fun. I am, but I will leave before the party **dies,**
make a believable excuse and find the exit. I don't mind being social, **but**
small talk feels like a coffin. My personal space is a cathedral, **not**
a sidewalk, not a strip mall. It's not a place that **everybody**
gets to walk through. It's a garden. I water it, and everything here **lives.**

"HOPE I GOT SOME BROTHERS THAT OUTLIVE ME" — DRAKE

Today, the opacity of my smile is at 3%, and I have a lot more rage than **hope**.
I grit my teeth and ball my fist until it forgets the word *peaceful*. Right now, **I**
am ready to punch the first thing that has the audacity to tell me that I ain't **got**
400 years' worth of reasons to be a chainsaw and wish somebody wood. **Some**
of you will unhinge your mouth, say we are all sisters and **brothers**,
and I will respond, *then you should be just as mad as I am **that***
officers are killing members of our family. All I want to do is **outlive**
racism and leave the house without my mother worrying about **me**.

"I'M JUST SAYING YOU COULD DO BETTER" — DRAKE

She has moved on and I see how bright she is in her new pictures. Now, **I'm** trying my best to explain to my future that most of its clothes are **just** too small. In six months, I outgrew all the plans I made and instead of **saying,** *She isn't coming back*, I look in the mirror, gather myself, and say, *You are worth coming back to.* I understand that only means it **could** happen. *Could* and *will* have slightly different occupations, but they **do** similar work. However, the latter is always so much **better.**

"I LEARNED WORKING WITH THE NEGATIVES CAN MAKE FOR BETTER PICTURES" — DRAKE

Stumbles and mistakes are not foreign to people like you and **I**.
We fall, scrape, scab, and then ask the skin what it **learned.**
The bruises fade, the wounds close—proves the body is still **working,**
hasn't given up yet—owns a white flag but doesn't know what to do **with**
the fabric. *Perseverance* is the kind of beauty I hope will stay so long that **the**
roads call it by its government name. Where every day feels like two **negatives**
sitting next to each other. We survive simply because we **can.**
Fortunately, it's the only thing we know how to **make.**
The recipe is complicated, but maybe this is all we're here **for.**
Maybe every loss makes the victory taste a little **better.**
Maybe life is a series of crashes, climbs, and smiling for **pictures.**

"I JUST TAKE MY TIME WITH ALL THIS; I STILL BELIEVE IN THAT" — DRAKE

I know eventually the hourglass runs out of sand. **I**
know eventually my chest will choose silence and **just**
stop making noise. Now, I remind myself not to **take**
this for granted. The weeks are moving faster, and **my**
goal is to breathe and enjoy the scenery because **time**
is the only vehicle that doesn't have brakes. It moves **with**
its own agenda and will not ask if you can keep up. **All**
thirty-nine years of me are tired, but what I know is **this:**
my smile is undefeated. My tragedy will not win. **I**
have bad days, but my good ones are stronger. I'm **still**
fighting the urge to skip to the end of the film. **I believe**
I'm here for a reason. Even when I don't know what to do **in**
this body, it has a purpose. I, at least, know **that.**

"JEALOUSY IS JUST LOVE AND HATE AT THE SAME TIME"
— DRAKE

The slowest brand of poison is **jealousy.**
It burrows deep inside the chest and **is**
often unrecognizable for years. Mostly **just**
lies quiet, uses an occasional outburst as a **love**
language. Dreams an alternate ending **and**
plays it over and over until it begins to **hate**
reality. Burns the toast and blames everyone **at**
the table. Breaks a wine glass and screams at **the**
breeze. Prays for your collapse with the **same**
mouth that calls you *friend* and asks for your **time.**

IV.

CONTRAPUNTAL

"We choose to believe, even when life speaks otherwise."

— KYLE "GUANTE" TRAN MYHRE, "BTS 40K: A CONTRAPUNTAL POEM"

CONTRAPUNTAL

The contrapuntal is considered a highly challenging and also highly flexible form. Created by writing two or more independent poems that can be read independently or together as a single poem, contrapuntal poems tend to be complex and give rise to surprising and layered meanings.

The form takes its name from the musical term, which means "of or in counterpoint," and refers to pieces of music that have two or more layered melodies.

One common approach to the contrapuntal is to write a pair of poems that can be read separately and then read together as a third poem when placed side by side, such that the individual first lines become one unified first line, and so on.

After attempting the golden shovel, the contrapuntal felt like the next logical step in this excursion. I was introduced to the form during Porsha Olayiwola's performance at the 2021 Stone Wall Poetry Slam. The entire audience sat up in our chairs when Porsha's name was announced. Porsha is one of the most dynamic poets in our scene, so we all knew we were going to see something special. I wondered if they were going to do a crowd favorite or if they would do something new. Porsha introduced their poem as a contrapuntal.

I was vaguely familiar with the form but had never seen one. I wondered how it would transfer to the stage, and shortly, that question was answered. The performance was absolutely captivating. The first and second poems were brilliant, and the third brought it all together in a surprising and genius culmination. After seeing this, I had to try it for myself.

Structurally, the contrapuntal is a puzzle. Attempting to make it all make sense frustrated me for days. I wanted all three poems to be good standalone works, but it was difficult to make each poem good while simultaneously joining them to tell a story. This was truly trial and error. Rearranging words to create multiple meanings really pushed me outside of my comfort zone. I found myself writing differently to fit the structure, and it turned out to be a great exercise that forced me to think of poetry as a malleable vehicle.

THE START

I know nervousness so well
I whistle and it comes running
because we are old friends
the first step is a stir of bravery
a creation in bloom a genesis a birth
the scariest thing I've ever done is begin

I call *anxious* by its first name
its ears perking at the sound of my voice
starting is a ritual of sweaty palms
a ceremony of courage
the reason why there is a story
the best thing I've ever done is begin

A PRAYER

May your blessings arrive early enough
and catch your sadness off guard
may tragedy be a step too slow
may forgiveness show up at your door
let every moment be a reminder that
a sunrise is still beautiful
and so are you

May joy appear in a flash flood
and call depression a liar until it shrinks
may regret loosen its grip
until shame is a language your body has forgotten
you are more than the sum of your mistakes
no matter how bad a day is it's allowed to start over
this is a direct order to continue shining

SAM

Samuel Francisco is
half-man half-forest fire
the scariest part of my childhood
all claws and criticism
now he is a friendly ghost

My father
a limping freight train with too much cargo
I remember him as a shadow with teeth
but now he is a clumsy beam of light
that doesn't remember the haunt

THE PHOTO

Today I found a picture of my parents
tucked inside a tattered box
a couple of young immigrants
breaking the elation into equal parts and sharing laughter
caught off guard on a Friday or perhaps a Saturday
my inheritance just having a good evening
like love is the only thing wedged between them
proof that they were happy once

A photograph of Sam and Val
hiding face down underneath a medley of knickknacks
my first two homes split funny down the middle
because there was too much for one person
all smiles wine and 70s fashion
a candid of them enjoying each other's company
joined at the hip
I hardly recognize them

BEFORE, AFTER, AND AFTER THAT

Somehow I have fallen in love with
the memory of your hands
an allowance of fingerprints
dancing on my skin even after you were gone
my heart a trembling beaker
hoping the experiment is gentle
I don't know the science of this
I heard something of chemicals
I read that smell is a time machine
and the body never forgets

The way you left me empty
clinging to the windows of a daydream
that held me longer than you did
my chest is just a petri dish
pretending to be a shot glass
I miss you the way fog misses the sky
but I know gravity never has good news
and that grief bumps into people on accident
mourning is the slowest vehicle in the world
I fear that I will be ironing you out of my smile forever

V.

QUESTION-AND-ANSWER

"The greatest compliment that was ever paid me was when one asked me what I thought, and attended to my answer."

— HENRY DAVID THOREAU, "LIFE WITHOUT PRINCIPLE"

QUESTION-AND-ANSWER

Question-and-answer poems come in many varieties, but most utilize a two-part structure in which the poem is divided into a question and its response. One approach is to pose a question in the title, with the body of the poem as the answer. Some question-and-answer poems read almost like riddles, revealing some correct answer to a series of questions; others simply pose successive questions in place of answers.

Poets use the form as a way of reflecting on their own experience, asking "what if" questions about society or history.

Much of the strength of the form comes from the simplicity and accessibility of conversational language. It is that same ease with which readers can navigate these poems that can give them their surprising depth and nuance.

Once, while I was scrolling Instagram, I saw that a friend of mine had posted a short poem. It began with a question, and the rest of the poem was the answer.

Many of us are writing about the same topics; what differentiates them is our personal experiences and how we approach the subject matter. Many writers do their best to avoid clichés, but I believe that despite something being used over and over, it never stops being relatable.

Instead of avoiding clichés completely, I take the spirit of the cliché and figure out how to make it feel new.

This form is an innovative way to repackage clichés and make them feel new. Instead of beginning the poem with a clever introduction, ask yourself a question such as, *How are you feeling?*, *How's life?*, *Did you eat today?*, and then use the poem to develop the answer.

WHY ARE YOU STILL IN BED?

Because going outside is expensive.
Because I spoke to people yesterday,
and I can't do that two days in a row.
Because I'm tired of living through
historical events.

Because unprecedented times
are starting to feel normal.

Because this morning, I made
a list of all my top priorities—

I'm one of them.

WHAT IS GROWTH?

I think of
the things
I was once
trembled about,

and laugh
quietly.

HOW DO YOU KNOW THAT YOU'RE HEALING?

I could have spent
the entire day
angry about this.

Instead, I don't
allow my problems
to speak

when my peace
has so much more
to say.

HOW DO YOU KNOW THIS IS LOVE?

I prefer being alone,
but now,

I want to do that
with you

as well.

WHAT IS PROGRESS?

There's a gap
between who I am
and who I want to be,

but every day
I watch it become
a little smaller.

WHAT'S YOUR TOXIC TRAIT?

Whenever I've gone
too long without sadness,
my brain tries to find
a little bit of it

somewhere.

WHY ARE YOU STILL IN BED?

Because it's been a rough year,
and it's only June.
Because it's been a rough week,
and it's only Monday.
Because it's been a rough day,
and it's only 10 a.m.

Because lately all my favorite
memories are here,

and sometimes,
you have to turn the day off,
turn it back on again,

and hope it's fixed.

VI.

FREE VERSE

"It is a fact that bumblebees have hair on their eyeballs
and people also should comb through everything they see"

— ANDREA GIBSON, "A LETTER TO THE PLAYGROUND BULLY
FROM ANDREA, AGE 8¾"

FREE VERSE

The history of poetry is frequently wrapped up with rhyme schemes, syllable counts, and specific forms. Much of contemporary poetry eschews some or all of these poetic structures and devices and instead fits into the category of free verse.

This style of poem ranges from the prose-like to the experimental. Some have no apparent concern for the placement of words on the page or larger structural concerns such as rhyme or rhythm while others meticulously construct and defy their own rules or push the boundaries of readers' expectations for poetry.

Poetry in free verse is an approach to writing unchained by formal constraints. It is less a form than it is an exploration of what is possible without form or at form's fringes.

Free verse is my first love. My introduction to poetry consisted of men who did not live in my era and did not look like me. I began thinking that people who come from neighborhoods like mine, people who looked the way that I do and spoke the way I spoke, didn't write poems.

I was a second-year college student when I first found poetry that I connected with. After a canceled class, my friend Antione and I headed to our friend Sadiq's dorm. On the TV was a brown-skinned man with a ponytail, speaking passionately about love. He'd say "I want a love like..." and finish the sentence with the kind of love he was looking for.

I don't remember if I sat down or if I stood up the entire time. I can't recall much about that hour of my life, but what I do remember is Mos Def was the host of the show. He called up performers, and they shared their stories in a way that had me completely enamored. At the end, Mos Def said, "Thank you for coming to Def Poetry."

I didn't know poetry could sound like that, look like that, and feel like that. It was both brand new and familiar. It was the first time I experienced poetry and wanted to be a participant. It was free of meters and rules. The only law was *be honest*, and I was ready to write about feelings that I never shared with anyone.

Six years later, that first poet I had seen when I walked into Sadiq's dorm would become my mentor, big brother, and friend, Shihan Van Clief.

I THINK I'M READY TO SIDE WITH TOMMY,

say that he had it right this whole time.

Though decades late,
I'm finally telling my teenage self
that it's ok to have a crush on Pam.

I tell him, *I see what's happening
here.* How you swallow a swarm of
butterflies every time you see her face
on the screen, and there is no shame in that.

Martin spends five seasons calling her
everything except attractive, and I regret
the amount of time it took for me to
come to her defense.

My friends fawn over Gina,
laugh when Pam is referred to as
BDB, and I say nothing.

Eight years later, the light-skin girl
shows up to the party, and Pavlov
rings the bell.

I wonder if this is how colorism
gets its meals.

It gathers the jokes we make about
each other,

and turns them into enough
food to survive for generations.

THESE DAYS,

I remind myself
that anger is a feeling
and not a lifestyle.

I'M THE KIND OF PERSON

that will *what if?*
a situation until
all the steam is gone,

will think about the
soup until it's cold
and then stomach
the after.

I've been known
to debate myself
into a corner

and call it home.

EVERY DAY, I GIVE UP

for twenty minutes

but decide to
push through
on the twenty-first.

Survival is a ritual,
a ceremony, and
a practice.

FRAGILE

I know the heart
can be a fragile and
dangerous thing.

When it breaks,
the ends are often jagged
and will cut the hands of people
who are just trying to help you
clean up the mess.

But I also know that
pain is nomadic. It
doesn't like to stay in
one place for too long.

Healing is a slow crawl,
but it will find you

right where you are.

TODAY, I TOLD A JOKE TO MYSELF

and laughed so hard
that it made all the silence
in the room uncomfortable.

The quiet left immediately,
said it didn't feel safe around
so much bliss.

The only things that stayed
were me and all this joy.

Is there a better way to live?

THERE AREN'T ENOUGH SONGS

about minding your own business
or staying home on a Saturday
because you think most people
are exhausting,

but I do believe that
we deserve an anthem.

An ode with a catchy hook
and beat by DJ Mustard.

Something we can dance to
after the plans we regret making
are canceled at the last minute.

Whenever the weekend
is visited by the patron saint
of empty schedules, we throw
a party in his honor

but only invite ourselves.

WHY SOME PEOPLE BE MAD AT ME SOMETIMES

After Lucille Clifton and FreeQuency

Because they don't get to decide
whether or not I have
a good enough reason to smile.

Because I'm joyful
without their permission.

Because I'm better
than my worst days.

Because I'm bigger
than my worst moments.

Because I forgave myself,
even though they didn't.

Because I love me,
even though they don't.

Because I root for them.
Because I pray for them—

still.

SO LET THEM

be wrong about us,

and let us not care
enough to correct them.

Let them grit their teeth
until their mouths are full of sand;

let them create a new beach
whenever they say our names.

Smile
and wave.

JUDGMENT IS A TRAIN

that is always on time.

I know exactly when
it's coming.

I can hear it rumble
from miles away,

but luckily, it's not
my only mode of
transportation.

NOW, I ONLY

surround myself
with people
who feel like
sunlight.

MY FRIENDS ARE SO GOOD

at saving my life
at least once a month
without even trying.

Sometimes, instead of saying *thank you,*
I just show up when they need me.

I feel like that means the same thing.

FORTY-FIVE YEARS LATER,

my mother's accent
still grapples with English.

Wrestles the language
until both parties
are exhausted and
agree to call it a draw.

Her accent is a good trouble,
a resistance that seems to
only get stronger with time.

When my mother speaks,
her voice becomes
the last train in the station.

My only way home.

BECAUSE THAT'S HOW WE'VE ALWAYS DONE IT

is a dangerous excuse.

You will think of
how the smoke
first seemed harmless,

and how the alarm
is unreliable and *acts up*
when the stove is on.

It will leave you
standing in ashes
thinking of all the ways
you could've
extinguished the fire.

JULY 4TH

I get it,
you love fireworks
and the way
they dance in the sky,

but some of the men in my family
still have war underneath
their fingernails,

ghosts that resurrect
in the belly of loud noises.

WHAT I OWE THE MIRROR

I hope you have the bandwidth
for forgiveness

and enough room in your palms
to fit an apology.

I saw you drowning,
watched your arms
confetti into the water,
and I only gave you feedback.

Heard you yell *fire*
and showed up with gasoline
just to see if you
could survive the furnace.

I should have been softer with you.
Could have held you differently.

I'm sorry for all the devastation
I created in the name of tough love.

ON HAPPINESS

I draw a stick figure,
and it kinda looks
like a spider,

but I'm okay with that.

I play my daughter's ukulele,
and the strings want to know
what they did to deserve
this category of torture.

It doesn't sound very good,
but that's fine.

I sing Whitney Houston songs
until my voice fractures.
Bludgeon the lyrics until
they are unrecognizable,

but I am not ashamed.

I'm teaching myself
about the opposite
of excellence,

the subtle art
of stumbling,

the radical act of failure
and forgiveness.

I'm learning
that embarrassment
only shows its face
if I allow it.

ON FATHER'S DAY

Today,
I do not use this energy
to critique my father
or his father
for what they did
and for what they didn't do.

Instead, I say,
Blessed be the broken cycle,
even though it must begin

here.

OF ALL THE HOODS

I hold my daughter
the same way
I hold my breath
during turbulence.

I patchwork
a bedtime story
and kiss her hands
before she falls asleep.
I call my mother
and say,

I get it now.
I finally understand.

UNTITLED

I hope you
stumble into
the kind of love

that bends all
the question marks
into exclamation points.

VII.

PAGE TO STAGE

"The first time that I discovered spoken word poetry on YouTube, that was like making best friends with the voices in my head."

— JOE LIMER, "POETRY"

PAGE TO STAGE

The term "page to stage" is not exclusive to poetry and refers to the decisions and strategies to create or adapt written work for theatrical performance. In poetry, the term commonly refers to preparing written texts for performance in front of a live audience.

One simple example of the page to stage process is practicing the performance of poetry crafted first for print publication. This process is generally focused on clarity of speech, pacing, emotional expression, and crowd engagement.

A more complex set of examples can be found in spoken word and performance poetry, where some poets begin by thinking about the stage and then work their way to the page. For performance poets, the process can involve stage cues, complex movement including dance and acrobatics, music, multiple performers, and a wide variety of other theatrical elements.

Regardless of the approach, performance poetry as a medium has advantages and disadvantages: it allows for movement, body language, vocal intonation, and direct experience of the author's emotional presence, but it also limits the listener's ability to re-read, slow down, or imagine their own version of events.

For the performing poet, trying to figure out how to use the strengths of both page and stage to their fullest is a challenging and creative process.

It's the year 2003. I'm a twenty-one-year-old fourth-year student at Alliant International University. It's a random Tuesday, and we are in San Diego, California. Claire de Lune, a popular coffee house on University Avenue, is hosting its weekly open mic. The room has approximately forty chairs, but there are about eighty people here, and the ratio is making personal space nearly impossible.

The MC says, "Next on stage, we have Rudy Francisco." Immediately, all the air inside my lungs takes a vacation, my hands tremble, and my heart is beating against my chest like it wants to be released. The ten-second walk to the stage feels like it's taking hours—a nervous pilgrimage with an audience at the end of the journey. I get in front of the microphone, and a poem spills out of my mouth—that was the moment my life turned in a very different direction.

I have developed an affinity for the written word, the nuances around deciding line breaks and rearranging text to give the poem a unique effect, but performance has a special place in my heart. When you listen to a poem being performed by the author, you have the opportunity to hear how the poem was intended to sound, providing further insight into the overall message.

People often ask me the difference between a performance poem and a page poem. In my experience, when I write for the page, I'm more concerned with visual aesthetics. I ask myself if the poem looks clean on the page, if the line breaks allow the reader to consume the poem in the desired cadence. I gift myself the option of not overly explaining everything, and I can take moments to challenge the reader to figure out anything in the text that isn't straightforward.

When writing a performance poem, I'm thinking of how the poem will sound out loud, how it feels when I say the words, syllable count, and rhythm. I also consider how I'm explaining the story. In performance, the audience will only be able to hear it once, so I provide details that will help the listener easily understand the narrative.

ORVILLE

A letter from Orville to Wilbur
the evening before their first flight:

The Wright Brothers,
Orville and Wilbur,
are known as the first engineers
to successfully design, build,
and operate an aircraft.

Brother,
last week,
I overheard a joke:
What do you call
two men who think they can fly?

A funeral.
To be honest, I didn't think it was funny either.

The whole town has become
an ocean of pointed fingers.

People I once called friends
are now just a tidal wave of unsolicited advice.
They're trying to rinse out the color from our dreams.

Yesterday, a lady from church pulled me aside
and said,
If God wanted us in the sky,
He would have given us wings.

And I replied, *Isn't that what imagination is?*
The act of actually going somewhere
that others can only think of?

Brother, sometimes,
people who have never even tried to run a mile
will tell you that a marathon is too far.

Some people will try to talk you out
of jumping into the water

simply because they have
always been too scared to learn how to swim.

Fear is when the brain digs out all faith from the body
and then calls it survival.

Fear is when we turn up the volume on
everything that might go wrong
and then allow it to speak louder than our courage.

But for those who do not worship at the altar of panic,
for those who will not sacrifice their ambitions
to a demigod of worst-case scenarios,
for those who do not give up,
failure is just a short story they tell
before they talk about success.

I know this process has been difficult.
The miscalculations, the hours we've put in,
the days we spend away from our families.

But every time I walk outside,
I can feel the ground getting nervous,
like it knows it cannot keep us here much longer
because we are destined for a higher calling.

I hear them say *it's impossible,*
but I say *everything is until it's not.*

They call us *stupid*.
I say *stupid and brave are just two sides of the same coin.*
The only difference is whether you guess correctly
before the penny hits the floor.

Tomorrow,
we will call gravity a liar.
We will kiss God on the face.
Tomorrow, I will look you in the eyes,
and I will say,
I told you the wind would feel different up here.

What they think does not matter.
When we are in the clouds,
we won't even be able to see them.

Brother,
I have a joke.
What do you call the first
two men in the world
who figure out how to fly?

Legends.

IN THE VOICE OF MY MOTHER'S WEDDING RING

Hey,
I'm not really sure where I am right now.
I think this is a drawer
or a cabinet.
All I really know is

it's dark here,
and I don't get out much these days.

Sometimes, my memory is a rusty anchor.
It drags a little every now and then,
but it does stop me from floating away.
What I'm saying is,
I know your parents.

Met your father when he was thirty,
and if I recall correctly,
it was the middle of the week,
an afternoon.

I had just gotten to the store that day;
I didn't even introduce myself to the rest of the jewelry,
because why?

Rings like me,
we don't stick around too long,
so what's the point of trying to make friends here?
The locket
was talking too much,
the watches kept staring,
the bracelets were all weirdos.
There was a promise ring next to me,

and I was like, *do people even buy those anymore?*
Like how long you have even been here?
But then
your dad shows up.

He arrived like early spring after a tough winter,
his mouth became a daffodil in July,
unfurled when he saw me,
and he said, *That's the one.*

When he gave me to your mother,
her eyes became two fireworks
in the night sky of her face.
When she said *yes*,
I knew this is what I was
created for.

But that was a long time ago.
Before the divorce,

I was on her finger for thirty-five years,
and during that time,
I watched alcohol and PTSD
scrape the smile off your father's face.
I saw him use his fists
when he couldn't locate
the right words.

And I tried to stop him,
but what is a ring supposed to do
in a situation like that?

I've been feeling guilty this whole time;
I still think it's my fault,
and now,
she can't even look at me.

So, I just sit in here
alone all day.

What I'm really trying to say is
if you find the right woman,
and you decide to spend your life with her—

I know this is going to sound silly
because the new rings are so nice,
and they're shinier than I am—

but all I need is a little polish,
a good home,
a second chance.

HOW THE SAUSAGE IS MADE

There is a common phrase
in the English language.

*You don't want to know
how the sausage is made.*

Meaning
there are things in life that we enjoy,
but if we saw the process it takes
to create them,

we might be shocked, frightened,
and they would be considered less desirable.

Meaning
it's harder to put food in your mouth
when you know the journey
it went through to get there.

Meaning
sometimes, mystery
makes it a little easier to handle.
Makes everything taste a little better.

And me,
some days I'm the food,
some days I'm the fork.
On both days, I'm just hoping
I'm good enough to be at the table,

and maybe
this is why I don't open up to people.

I'd rather be a page with no browser history,
a conveyor belt with no baggage.

So, when you tell me I'm funny,
I don't tell you that, somehow, trauma
made me find humor in strange places.

When you compliment my achievements,
I don't say *I'm still trying to prove to myself*

that I'm worth all the oxygen I'm taking
from the atmosphere.

A FEW THINGS

On days like this,
I think of all things I could be,
and I choose to be happy.

On days like this,
I think of all the accessories
I could wear and I choose
a smile.

On days like this,
I think of all the names
I could call myself
and I say "Grateful"
"Worthy"
I say "Still here"

On days like this,
my mind, my body and spirit
turn into a three-piece band
and they are playing
all their greatest hits

like "Joy", and "Laughter"
And "Letting go of anything
that doesn't make me feel like
The best version of myself."

I don't know much,
but I know a few things about a broken heart,
it's probably the worst injury you can have,
it happens to us all
but it won't last forever.

I know a few things about revenge,
it doesn't change what already happened
and it won't make the pain go away.

Revenge is like starving yourself
while making a meal for someone
who isn't even hungry.

it's like holding your breath
and hoping all your enemies
run out of oxygen.

I know a few things about forgiving,
it's harder than it looks,
but it feels a lot better than it sounds.

I heard,
while leaving Sodom,
Lot's wife wanted to see what was
happening, turned around and
was transformed into a pillar of salt

I know a few things about leaving,
if you take too much time packing your stuff,
you'll convince yourself
to stay longer than you planned,
but when you finally do it,
don't look back.

I know a few things about letting go,
it doesn't always seem like the best idea,
but it's for your own safety.

I know a few things about healing,
it's not a good employee.

it shows up when it's ready
and only works when it wants to.

I know a few things about self care;
it's not as fancy as looks on Instagram.

Sometimes, it looks like laying down.
Sometimes, it looks like drinking a glass of water.
Sometimes, it's playing your favorite song
and dancing like the room is on fire,
but you are an ice cube that does not know how to melt.

I know a few things about my body.
It's the only one I have
and it becomes everything I say it is,

My body does not like to raise its voice.
It doesn't like to ask to rest more than once
and if you don't listen,
it'll go on strike when I need it the most.

I know a few things about my mind.
It's the most powerful tool that I own.
If I think I am,
then I will be
and I'll of my success
begins with what I choose to believe
about myself.

I know a few things about my spirit.
It's not something I can point to
or draw a picture of
but I know it's there.
I can feel it when I breathe
and it holds me together

on days when I feel like
falling apart.

I know a few things about life;
being human is difficult,
being a good human is even harder,
but it's still something
I would like to accomplish while I'm here.

I know a few things about myself,
I hate mustard, I'm scared of raccoons
and I've made a lot of mistakes,

but I know a few things about tomorrow,
it's kind of like a shadow.

It's hard to see when the sun isn't bright,
but regardless,

it's there.

It's always there,
like the moon and the stars.
Sometimes, I look up at the night sky
and I'm reminded that people and planets
aren't so different;

we all have an orbit,
our energy decides
what comes into our atmosphere,
we all have our own gravity.

HIDE AND SEEK

My daughter is seven years old,
and right now, her favorite game
is hide and seek.

The funny part is
she always tells me where to hide.

She says, *You go right here,*
I'll count, and then I'll come find you.

I know—
that's not how the game is played.
I'm supposed to find a good spot,
hide behind a door, a couch,
or inside a closet.

I'm supposed to make her
look around the house,
and try to figure out exactly where I am.
I don't do any of that

because I know what it feels like
to wonder where your father is.

Thinking, *I know he has to be here, somewhere.*
I come from a long line of boys
who had to pick out their own razors
and teach themselves how to shave.

A lineage of young men
who threw footballs in the air
and watched them land on the ground.

We are echoes in a cave
trying to love the frequency of our noise
but have no idea where it comes from.

The first time I got an A on a test,
I whispered, *I'm proud of you*, to myself
just so I could hear what it sounded like
in a man's voice.

The first time I scored a touchdown,
my football coached hugged me,
and I said, *Thanks, Dad*, on accident.

I've copied and pasted my father into
all of my best moments, and then felt guilty
for not appreciating him for showing up.

It's fascinating how the mind will do backflips
if you just give it enough time to stretch.

To be honest,
I thought this feeling was a
pair of hand-me-down jeans:
something too big for me right now,
but a garment I would grow into
and then out of as I got older.
But here I still am,
trying to be a father to my daughter
and myself.

And this is usually the part of the story when
I say I don't know who my dad is.
I'll tell you I could look at five different pictures
and not know who is responsible
for half of my DNA,

but did you know
that distance and proximity
can eat at the same table?

Did you know
that a house can feel like an entire planet,
and silence can turn two rooms into countries
on opposite sides of the world?

Silence is my first language,
and lonely is an accent
that I can't seem to get rid of.

I was told
my father left for the Vietnam War,
but only his body came home.
I have no idea who he was before
PTSD grabbed him by the happiness.

My dad
is one of the many rocks that America
threw at another country,
and eventually that country
decided to throw him back.

But every day, I saw a ghost open my front door,
walk right through me without flinching,
and my entire childhood
felt like an event that has no RSVPs.

Once, a friend said,
At least your father didn't leave you.
And I replied,
At least yours only did it once.

They say
the apple always falls close to the tree.
But if someone picks it up,
it'll go as far as they do.
Luckily, it's my daughter's favorite fruit.

So, when she says,
let's play hide and seek,
I say, *yes.*

When she says,
wait right there,
I say, *yes.*

When she says,
Dad, you're so easy to find,

I say,
yea, I'm always right here.

A SERIES OF GENTLE REMINDERS

Delete the number,
trash the boxes,
give the sweaters away.
Stop holding onto things
that do not fit you anymore.
Clutter has many faces.

Forgive them.
They didn't apologize,
and you're still mad,
but what I do know is this:
a closed fist
can punch through a wall,
but you can't fix the hole
until you open your hands.

The past
is one of the few things
more stubborn than we are.
It will not change
and doesn't care if
you have a better idea
of how the story
should've ended.

Healing begins
when we stop trying to run
backwards on the escalator
and embrace whatever will
keep us moving forward.

It's hard
being alive,
but it looks
so good on you.
Someone is happy
that you exist.

So many things have
tried to break you.
None of them turned in
their assignments.
I think that's a good
reason to celebrate.
I heard it only takes
one person to be a parade.

The truth is
we aren't here long enough
to drag around this much apathy.

Pluck a ream of smiles
from any place that has
a few extra laying around.
Stash one for yourself
and give the rest away
because some of us
are chewing on our last
spoonful of hope,
and sometimes, kindness
can feel like a full stomach.

Tell people you love them
while they can still hear you
because death doesn't call
before it comes over.

Time will agree to play freeze tag
but will follow none of the rules.

Hey,

try not to be so hard on yourself.
We don't know how long we'll be on this planet
or what we're supposed to do while we're here.
We're all just crashing into each other
and trying to fall in love with the collision.

VIII.

LOVE POEMS

"You might think you know me, but if you ain't never seen me with her, you ain't never seen me alive."

— TAALAM ACEY, "SHE CONJUREZ"

LOVE POEM

Love poetry is the workhorse of the poetic canon. The best known, the most universal, widely loved or widely maligned.

Love poems often communicate some specific aspect of being in love and tend to have a universality that goes beyond the writer.

While the romantic love poem is often thought of as the paragon of the form, work written about family, spirituality, and the self are also celebrated topics for love poetry.

It could be said that all poetry is love poetry. If you believe that attention is love, it is no great stretch to find love in the act of writing poetry. While there is no clear rule that says what can or cannot be a love poem, there is a familiar, if ineffable, quality—think of the poems that are read at weddings, or that young lovers write for one another.

If I had to name my favorite things about the '90's, music would have to be number one. At the time, rhythm and blues still had good knees, and men weren't too proud to beg a woman into forgiveness. They would challenge pneumonia to an altercation and dance shirtless in the rain for as long as it took the apology to have a steady pulse. Asking if her eyes were still green and wondering if she ever reached for him in the middle of the night.

Men cut themselves into groups of three to six, put on matching colors, and belted songs like they were trying to convince the universe to spill a few drops of good luck into their hands. They gave romance a little swagger and made love feel like something I wanted to participate in.

Once, in the middle of my rendition of "Can We Talk," my classmate Justin yelled out, "Aye, Rudy, who sings that song?" Thinking, *how does he not know this?* I replied, "Tevin Campbell," and he said, "Yeah...let's keep it that way."

As I grew older, I slowly realized that I would never be the songbird of my generation or the fifth member of Boyz II Men, or Dru Hill, or B2K, or 112, but something special happened when I found poetry.

Taalam Acey was the first poet I watched do a thirty-minute set. I saw him at R. Spot, a Black-owned barbershop and bookstore that hosted an open mic on Fridays. Taalam spoke with an intense urgency that made the audience hold their breath and cling to every statement. His punchlines made the crowd members exclaim, "Say that!" and "Talk to 'em!" The experience was a cross between church and concert, and I left inspired.

Prior to this experience, I had only heard Black men talk about love in songs, as if R&B gave us permission to be romantic without feeling corny. Soon, I realized that many Black men used spoken word as a vehicle to discuss a myriad of topics, including love. At this time, most of my poems were political. Much of my work was rooted in the plight of being Black in America, but being exposed to poems about love made me want to step outside of my comfort zone and explore that topic as well.

MAYBE YOU LEFT THE BOOKSTORE RIGHT BEFORE I GOT THERE.

Maybe you were two cars
behind me at the stoplight.

Maybe I got off the train
before you got on.

Maybe I transferred
to a school that you just left.

Maybe I moved into a house
next door to the house you moved out of.

Maybe we were both in an elevator
on opposite sides of the same building.

Maybe I've been three steps
behind you my whole life.

Maybe we are just two planets
in the same solar system,
hoping to find something in this galaxy
that will look at our eyes like they've
never seen two of them on the same face,
and think maybe we are magic.

Someone who will hear the forever in our laugh.
Someone who will see beauty in our mistakes.

Dear whoever you are,

on the day we finally meet,
I imagine there will be

static electricity in your voice.
Your name will be the sheet music
to a song I've been trying to play by ear,

and we will fall into each other
like two stars that are tired of the sky.

ALL THE FIREFLIES HAVE RETURNED

The leaves
are young,

and I think
the sunflowers
are rooting for us.

My chest is always
full of questions,
but your smile
is a good answer,

dependable as
the morning.

I hope someday
we can trust
each other
with our most
vulnerable stems,

and together, bloom
in all the right places.

SPEAKING OF PARADISE,

I saw your hands today

and wondered what
it would be like
to live there.

I SAID, *I LOVE YOU,*

and I know that
isn't enough.

Words are flour
and water, but
relationships
cannot survive
on bread alone.

I ONCE FELT SAD ABOUT FALLING STARS.

Seemed like such
an awful circumstance,

but now,
your voice turns my
entire face into a garden.

You make me feel like
the kind of harvest
that only comes from
good soil.

I, too, would trade
the sky for this.

AFTER JEFFREY McDANIEL

In an effort to eradicate
meaningless conversation,

the government
has passed a new law:

from now on,
all greetings—*hello*, *hi*,
hey, and *wassup*—
have been replaced
with the phrase, *I love you*.

When a stranger is lost
they say *I love you*
before they ask for directions.

The cashier at the grocery store
says, *I love you* before
Paper or plastic?

It's the first thing a child hears
when they are born.

All conversations have
a tender urgency.

A soft importance.

I love you
before anything else.

There is no more small talk.

ACKNOWLEDGMENTS

Shihan, thank you for being the first person to inspire me to write poetry. You made a career as a spoken word artist tangible.

Javon, thank you for constantly pushing me. Thank you for being a brother, advisor, mentor, and friend. I owe you more than I could ever pay back.

Joel Francois, thank you for constantly reminding me of who I am and encouraging me to remember my worth.

Alma Rodriguez, thank you for believing in me all these years. Thank you for allowing me to use Queen Bee's and being our poetry community's lifeline.

Mom, thank you for supporting me, raising me, loving me. I hope someday I get to take care of you the same way you've taken care of me.

Zoey, you are my biggest inspiration. I hope someday you look at what I've been able to achieve, and I make you proud.

Button, thank you again for allowing me to publish with you. I'm grateful for all the time and energy you have put into my work. I am endlessly grateful for our partnership.

NOTES IN ORDER OF APPEARANCE

'Excuse Me As I Kiss the Sky' comes from Method Man's "How High (Remix)" and is a riff off of the Jimi Hendrix line ''Scuse me while I kiss the sky' from the song "Purple Haze."

Junious "Jay" Ward, "An Ode to What the Divorce Didn't Take" was published by Button Poetry on December 13, 2022.

Victoria Chang, "Tankas" comes from Chang's collection *Obit*, published by Copper Canyon Press on April 07, 2020.

Terrance Hayes, "The Golden Shovel" comes from Hayes' collection *Lighthead*, published by Penguin Books on March 30, 2010.

"Everybody dies, but not everybody lives" is a lyric from Drake's verse in Nicki Minaj's 2010 hit "Moment 4 Life," featured on her debut album, *Pink Friday*.

"Hope I got some brothers that outlive me" is a lyric from Drake's song "God's Plan" off the 2018 album, *Scorpion*.

"I'm just saying you could do better" is a lyric from Drake's song "Marvins Room" off the 2011 album, *Take Care*.

"I learned working with the negatives can make for better pictures" is a lyric from Drake's song "HYFR" off the 2011 album, *Take Care*.

"I just take my time with all this; I still believe in that" is a lyric from Drake's song "Headlines" off the 2011 album, *Take Care*.

"Jealousy is just love and hate at the same time" is a lyric from Drake's song "Over My Dead Body" off the 2011 album, *Take Care*.

Kyle "Guante" Tran Myhre, "BTS 40K: A Contrapuntal Poem" was published by KTM aka GUANTE on January 22, 2023.

Andrea Gibson, "A Letter to the Playground Bully from Andrea, age 8¾" was published by Andrea Gibson on June 01, 2011.

"why some people be mad at me sometimes" is inspired by Lucille Clifton's poem "why some people be mad at me sometimes" found in *The Collected Poems of Lucille Clifton 1965-2010* published by BOA Editions on August 28, 2012.

Joe Limer, "Poetry" was published by Sunday Jump on August 19, 2022.

Taalam Acey, "She Conjurez" was published by raschild1 on October 29, 2007.

After Jeffrey McDaniel is written after "The Quiet World," originally published in Jeffrey McDaniel's collection *Forgiveness Parade* published by Manic D. Press on October 01, 1998.

All section definitions courtesy of Button Publishing Inc.

ABOUT THE AUTHOR

Rudy Francisco is one of the most recognizable names in Spoken Word Poetry. At the age of twenty-one, Rudy completed his B.A in Psychology and decided to continue his education by pursuing a M.A in Organizational Studies. As an artist, Rudy Francisco is an amalgamation of social critique, introspection, honesty, and humor. He uses personal narratives to discuss the politics of race, class, gender, and religion, while simultaneously pinpointing and reinforcing the interconnected nature of human existence. Francisco is the author of two full-length poetry collections—*Helium* (Button Poetry, 2017) and *I'll Fly Away* (Button Poetry, 2020). Rudy was the first spoken word poet to perform on *The Tonight Show* with Jimmy Fallon and was most recently seen on ABC's *The Bachelorette* as the contestant's poetry coach.

BloodFresh **by Ebony Stewart**

BloodFresh by Ebony Stewart is a stunning collection of robust poems. This assembly of work gives the reader a glimpse into the details of the author's life while allowing the audience an opportunity to find pieces of themselves within the narratives. Ebony finds brilliant and lucid ways of discussing heavy topics and pairs them with beautiful moments of self-discovery. This book is about survival, celebration, and everything between.

A Peculiar People by Steven Willis

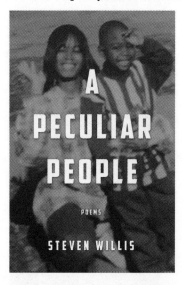

Steven Antoine Willis uses his craft to highlight the multidimensional nature of Blackness by pairing politics with personal experience. *A Peculiar People* is succinct and focused, addressing a wide range of topics such as family, music, hardships, and sacrifice. This book is insightful, brave, humorous, and absolutely worth reading.

Composition by Junious "Jay" Ward

COMPOSITION

JUNIOUS WARD

Composition by Junious "Jay" Ward takes the reader on a scenic poetic journey. This collection highlights the various ways a poem can be written by exploring forms and using line breaks as a tool that also tells a story. Ward creates an engaging experience while tackling issues such as race, colorism, and grief. *Composition* is a breath of fresh air and a necessary addition to any poetry lover's bookshelf.

OTHER BOOKS BY BUTTON POETRY

If you enjoyed this book, please consider checking out some of our others, below. Readers like you allow us to keep broadcasting and publishing. Thank you!

Michael Lee, *The Only Worlds We Know*
Raych Jackson, *Even the Saints Audition*
Brenna Twohy, *Swallowtail*
Porsha Olayiwola, *i shimmer sometimes, too*
Jared Singer, *Forgive Yourself These Tiny Acts of Self-Destruction*
Adam Falkner, *The Willies*
George Abraham, *Birthright*
Omar Holmon, *We Were All Someone Else Yesterday*
Rachel Wiley, *Fat Girl Finishing School*
Bianca Phipps, *crown noble*
Natasha T. Miller, *Butcher*
Kevin Kantor, *Please Come Off-Book*
Ollie Schminkey, *Dead Dad Jokes*
Reagan Myers, *Afterwards*
L.E. Bowman, *What I Learned From the Trees*
Patrick Roche, *A Socially Acceptable Breakdown*
Rachel Wiley, *Revenge Body*
Ebony Stewart, *BloodFresh*
Ebony Stewart, *Home.Girl.Hood.*
Kyle Tran Mhyre, *Not A Lot of Reasons to Sing, but Enough*
Steven Willis, *A Peculiar People*
Topaz Winters, *So, Stranger*
Darius Simpson, *Never Catch Me*
Blythe Baird, *Sweet, Young, & Worried*
Siaara Freeman, *Urbanshee*
Robert Wood Lynn, *How to Maintain Eye Contact*
Junious 'Jay' Ward, *Composition*
Usman Hameedi, *Staying Right Here*
Sierra DeMulder, *Ephemera*
Taylor Mali, *Poetry By Chance*
Matt Coonan, *Toy Gun*
Matt Mason, *Rock Stars*
Sean Patrick Mulroy, *Hated for the Gods*

Available at buttonpoetry.com/shop and more!